Sophia, The Holy Spirit

Articles
concerning the Holy Spirit
as
Sophia, the Divine Feminine,
and
Female Spirituality

D1302300

by

La Ermita – The Hermitage

First publication September 2005
Revisited October 2018
La Ermita – The Hermitage
239 Orange Street
Macon, GA 31201
www.laermita.org

Table of Contents

Prologue

t was in 1994 that we of La Ermita-The Hermitage became aware that the Holy Spirit wanted to be known also as Sophia. It was not a sudden revelation because we had become aware that She was the feminine aspect of the Trinity in 1989. Little did we realize then that She was already known in many places of the world as Sophia, the Divine Feminine. In 1991 Carolyn Matthews published her textbook manual on *Sophia* in England. In 1997 Susanne Schaup published her German book, *Sophia*, in English.

St Paul wrote that the 'last days' belonged to the Holy Spirit. For him, the 'last days" referred to the period between Pentecost and the end of the world, which he thought was very close, but unfortunately, Sophia's life that She gave at Pentecost was short lived. She was soon controlled by those in authority and was not able to continue filling her children with love as She did at Pentecost. However, we truly believe that today Her time has arrived. We are in that moment of change.

This is truly Her Age, the Age of the Divine Feminine, Sophia, the Holy Spirit. Her gifts, especially those of love and compassion, are becoming visible, existing in both men and women equally. With Her gifts, the redemption earned by Jesus Her Son will truly transform this world into their Divine Family.

These articles are not presented as a theological thesis, rather as a sharing of what we learned in our personal mystical experiences during contemplative prayer with Her. We write simply what we have come to know, and what it has cost us as individuals who desired more inner healing so that we could be the Divine Love that we are. Sophia's love heals. She is a Mother, a sister, and a spouse who loves everyone. Love does not separate. May our thoughts and experiences bring a blessing to you as well.

Finally, we need to assure everyone that what we say concerning the Holy Spirit as the Divine Feminine does not have to be accepted. We are not proclaiming a new dogma of faith. People have saved their souls for centuries without knowing this, and they will continue doing so in the future. But for those who desire a deeper intimate love relationship, the acceptance of the Holy Spirit as the Divine Feminine opens that door of their heart. After all, loving all Three of Them is the first commandment.

If you wish to know more about us, you can find us at our website: www.laermita.org.

September 2005
Macon, GA

Why the Name Sophia?

La Ermita – The Hermitage is devoted to proclaiming the Holy Spirit as the Divine Feminine who wishes to be called Sophia or Mother Sophia. But before we share with you why the Holy Spirit is the Divine Feminine of the Blessed Trinity, let us first show why She wants to be known and called "Sophia" instead of "Holy Spirit."

Not too long ago we read an article that stated the Holy Spirit was the forgotten person of the Holy Trinity. The author put emphasis on the word "person." Why would he make such a statement when we all pray to the Holy Spirit? Is it true?

In our estimation, he was correct. There is a difference in the way we human beings relate to two of the divine persons, whom we know as our Heavenly Father and Jesus, than in the way we relate to the divine person we know as the Holy Spirit.

With the Father we have an image of fatherhood. It may not be the best of images because of our human fathers, but we know who a father is. Therefore, we can pray and relate to him as a Father because of our relationship to our human fathers. As a result, our relationship with Him can become very personal.

The same situation exists with the Son of God, whom we know as Jesus.

Jesus, the Son of God, became a man. He has a human body like ours, and as a result of being a human being like us, we have all kinds of wonderful images concerning Him, as our redeemer, savior, and brother. And so, when we pray and relate to Him, these images bring forth feelings and awareness that give us the ability to relate personally to Him.

But when we come to the Holy Spirit, the Third Person of the Trinity, we use words that are not expressing a human being.

How can we relate personally to an image of a 'spirit' as a person? 'Ghosts' images keep us at a distance. In fact, Holy Ghost was Her name for centuries.

7

We can imagine the Holy Spirit as 'power,' but how can we relate to power as a person?

We can imagine the Holy Spirit as a 'dove,' but how can we relate to a dove as a person.

We can imagine the Holy Spirit as a 'tongue of fire,' but how can we relate to a tongue of fire as a person?

None of these images are a person.

We have no problem loving God the Father as a person, no problem loving God the Son as a person because we have human images of them as a person, but when it comes to the Holy Spirit we do not have a human image that makes it easy for us to love Her as a person.

Obviously, She too has a right to be known and loved as a person just as the other two divine persons.

In order to help us arrive at that personal relationship with Her She has requested that we call Her Sophia instead of Holy Spirit.

Sophia is a Greek word for Wisdom, but in the world, it is also a woman's name, and that gives us a human connection.

In the five Books of Wisdom in the Old Testament we read that she is constantly called Sophia. So, it is not a new name, but rather her original name.

May these thoughts concerning Her name help us to experience a loving personal relationship, one that has the same type of feelings that we have towards our Father and Brother Jesus.

Why is the Holy Spirit the Divine Feminine?

We read in Genesis that God created us in their image and likeness. Male and female They created us. They also created us in a family that is composed of father, mother and children. Living in a family gives us lots of opportunities to grow in love because in a family all things are in common between us. We share all that we have with each other. And we are all equal even though we are each different.

All this is our very nature and was given to us because They create us to their image and likeness. It cannot be any other way, because They cannot create anything different than who They are. As God, all creation exists within their essence, but as a created point.

When we are baptized we are baptized formally into the Family of God, God the Father, God the Mother and God the Son. We Christians have always referred to the Trinity as the Family of God into which we are born again.

So, again, since we are made in the image and likeness of God, then what we possess naturally as social human beings also exists within them. God being infinite, nothing can exist outside of God.

It was Jesus who revealed to us that there were three persons in the Trinity. He told us that the first person was our Father and that He was the Son.

Now, if we have a Father and Son, there must be a Mother. But the only person left in the Trinity is the Holy Spirit. Therefore, the Holy Spirit must be God the Mother.

When we look at all the passages in Scripture concerning the Holy Spirit we notice that the Holy Spirit's activities are always those that pertain to the feminine.

For example, the Holy Spirit is constantly giving birth and nourishing one's soul and spirit. In other words, She is involved in the formation of Her child, be that the person Jesus or we human beings. That relationship began at both our physical and spiritual birth. That's why we are children of God.

The Holy Spirit gave birth to the church on Pentecost.

The Holy Spirit raised Jesus from the dead, giving him life again.

This characteristic of giving birth is not attributed to the Father nor to the Son. It is exclusively the work of the Holy Spirit, who is feminine.

The Holy Spirit feeds us with the food of the Father's creation and of Jesus' redemption. She forms us with her Gifts of the Spirit. She molds us into being beautiful children of Their Family, the Family of the Father, Mother Sophia and Son Jesus.

These are feminine characteristics that we know and experience in our human mothers. As a result, they also are Sophia's characteristics as the Holy Spirit because we are made to Their image and likeness.

It is for these reasons that we have come to know the Holy Spirit, Sophia, as the Divine Feminine of the Godhead.

This is especially good news for women. Now, they can know and understand that there is a Person in the Trinity that is like them, a Divine Person whom they can imitate. No longer are they commanded by the church to be like Jesus. He is a man and women need to be women.

But, Sophia is also good news for men as well, but that we will see later.

As we stated in the beginning, no one needs to accept this, but it does touch something deep within all of us, especially women, namely, the awareness that we *truly* are made to image and likeness.

We assure you that once you meet and know Sophia, the Divine Feminine, you will never regret it. May these thoughts lead you to a deeper love relationship and devotion not only with our Father and Jesus, the Son, but most of all with Sophia, the Holy Spirit.

Is Angel Sophia Truly Divine?

We read in the Book of Proverbs, Chapter 8, verses 22 and the following where Sophia says, "The Lord begot me, the firstborn of his ways, the forerunner of his prodigies of long ago…. When he set for the sea its limit, so that the waters should not transgress his command; then was I beside him as his craftsman, and I was his delight day by day."

If Sophia is the first of all God's creatures and especially His angelic beings, then how can She be the Holy Spirit, who is God?

The relationship here between the Holy Spirit and Sophia is similar to the relationship between the Second Person of the Trinity, the Son of God, and Jesus.

Let us explain this relationship.

The Second Person of the Trinity, who is the Son of God, took unto himself a body like ours and became man. That man is called and known as Jesus. What we have here is a union of the Second Person of the Trinity with a human nature. That means that Jesus has two natures, one is Divine, and the other is human. Two natures in one Person. It is his Person as the Son of God that dwells in his two natures, divine and human. And we express this union by saying "Jesus, the Son of God."

The same is true of the Holy Spirit and Sophia.

The Third Person of the Trinity, who is the Holy Spirit, took unto herself a created spirit of the angelic kingdom and was the first of all of them. That created Spirit is called and known in Scripture as Sophia. So, we have the union of the Third Person of the Trinity with a created angelic nature. That means that Sophia has two natures, one is divine, and the other is a created angelic nature. The Person of God is the Holy Spirit. This union of one Person with two natures we call by the name of "Sophia, the Holy Spirit," or "Mother Sophia."

Do we realize the loving significance of what is expressed here?

Our Heavenly Father dwells in all of creation as the creator. Sophia dwells in all of His creation as the Life giver and Mother, and Jesus dwells in all of

His human creation as the Brother Redeemer. All Three Persons are intimately and lovingly connected to and dwell within Their creation. No separation. Yet, we feel that they live up in the sky, out there somewhere. Separated.

Jesus shared this reality to us when he said that all three of Them wanted to dwell intimately within us. They are not a God who dwells somewhere out there in space. They lovingly dwell within us totally and completely.

But since that original unity of love ceased being visible with Adam and Eve, They want us to know that They still desire it to be the same. They desire that we open the door to their room within our spirit and invite Them to come and dwell within the "living, dining room and even the bedroom" of our spirit.

All three desire a personal relationship with us, a family relationship, and an intimate relationship. Each of them wishes to share their special love with us, and each one's love is different. One is the love of a Father, the other of a Mother, spouse or sister, and the other of a brother. We belong to their family. We are God's family.

Now we can understand what She said in Proverbs: "I, Sophia, was his delight day by day, playing before him all the while, playing on the surface of his earth; and I found delight in the sons of men." Yes, the angel Sophia is truly the Third Person of the Holy Trinity just as the man Jesus is truly the Second Person of the Holy Trinity.

May all of us come to experience and know this great and delightful love of Sophia, the Holy Spirit.

Why Have a Devotion to Sophia, the Holy Spirit?

We are all called to love the Lord our God with our whole heart and soul. Some people feel that a dedicated friendship love fulfills this commandment. But many others like the saints and mystics have expressed their loving relationship in terms of a spiritual marriage.

In the past, when a nun professed her first vows of dedication to the Lord, she presented herself dressed as a bride. She was spiritually marrying Jesus. If she took that relationship seriously, she would eventually experience in her soul and body the results of her spiritual marriage, an ecstasy of complete and total marital union with Jesus.

Other women, in general, may have difficulty experiencing a friendship love or a spiritual marital relationship because of their present human marriage.

Scripture in Genesis says that Eve came from Adam's side, and the interpretation of that Scripture for centuries has made it difficult for a woman to be who she is made to be.

However, women today are breaking away from masculine control, masculine remaking, and are demanding equality not only in our human family life but also in the life of the Divine Family of God, the Church.

We see this movement basically as part of Mother Sophia's work to re-establish her Family of Pentecost, but there is a tendency for some women to go the other extreme, namely, to adopt too many "masculine" characteristics as they seek equality. That's no good either. Here is where the relating to Sophia in prayer is beneficial for women. Sophia as God will teach and show them how to be truly a woman just as Jesus taught men how to be truly men.

But what about the men? What man would seek an intimate loving relationship with the Holy Spirit when he understands that all Three Persons of God have masculine characteristics? He would have no problem growing in a very strong personal friendship with Them, but a spiritual marital relationship of love would be much stronger.

Fortunately, when hetero men are able to open up to Sophia the Holy Spirit, the feminine part of the Trinity, then those who wish that deep intimate loving relationship with Her are able to arrive at it. Such a spiritual marital relationship will also strengthen their human marital relationship as well. Love does not separate.

However, fear of true and total intimacy in love is frightening for both men and women, probably more for men because in every man there exists a deep subconscious fear of surrendering to women. It keeps him from total abandonment to her. The fear is so deep that it probably goes back to Adam and Eve.

In other words, it would seem that man is still afraid that the present "Eve" will do him in completely once again. This fear has to be faced with love and healed both in one's human relationship as well as the divine.

Men must let go of these fears and give freedom to women, and especially, to Sophia, the divine feminine.

This is not at all easy even for the male clergy of most religions. Sophia is allowed freedom only when the sacraments are administered, or the Word is preached by an ordained minister. Since She is feminine She is not free to "blow where She will." She is not free to be a Mother who forms her children according to whom they are. She is not free to dwell in the marketplace.

St. Teresa of Avila says that the worst fear in everyone's life is the fear of entering the 7th Mansion, because a spiritual marriage is the climax of one's loving relationship with God. We all fear giving up totally our whole self to the other.

Once again, what is feared on the human marital level is also feared on the spiritual marital level.

These are some reasons for having a loving devotion to Sophia, the Holy Spirit, having a desire to be in an intimate loving relationship with the Third Person of the Trinity.

How can we live a devotion to Sophia?

In the previous article we learned the reasons for having a devotion to Sophia, the Holy Spirit. Now we would like to share about how we can express our love for and to Her.

First of all, we need to grow in our knowledge and awareness of Her by reading the Old and New Testament and meditating on what we noticed Her doing among Her Children in those days. As that is being done, then we need to turn our sight for something similar that is happening today. That will give us a connection with the past, and we will realize that She is here with us now as She was in those days.

But the second and best way is to spend time in silence each day if possible, in order to invite Her to visit us in our imagination. She will come. We will see Her. Once She is before us in our imagination, we just need to begin relating to Her. She will speak to us. She will bless us. She will help us. She will teach us.

This prayer is simple. We do not have to pray memorized prayers. We do not have to do anything more than invite Sophia to visit us in our imagination, and then wait for Her arrival.

If at any time we doubt that it is Sophia who is present and speaking to us, simply say, "let us kneel down together and pray the 'Our Father.' If it is Sophia, She will pray. If it is any kind evil spirit it will not pray. Evil will never pray. Then, we tell the evil to leave in the Name of Jesus, and Sophia will appear.

This is the prayer of the saints. It is also a prayer for us.

Jesus said: "I will love you and reveal myself to you." And again, "My Father will send in my name the Holy Spirit who will instruct you in everything and remind you of all that I told you." And remember what She said in Proverbs, that She delights to be with the children of God.

Finally, because of this loving relationship we will become aware that we are able to live and share Her Gifts that She has given us, especially the gift of love.

Let's not be afraid. Let's take a few quite moments each day and invite Sophia to visit us. Her delight will become ours!

The Shekinah, the Visible Presence of Sophia

In the Old Testament we read that after Moses built the temple the "Glory of the Lord" filled it with a cloud. This cloud was called "the Shekinah," which means, the visible manifestation of the Divine Spirit. In other words, the temple (masculine) was empty until it was filled by the Holy Spirit (feminine). The Father and Mother Sophia together created and visibly formed their home on earth in the temple.

And so, it is with us.

Our bodies are Their created physical structures, temples, that are given spiritual life by being filled with the Shekinah, the Holy Spirit. That experience of Her presence of love is what forms in us the feeling of being at "home" in our bodies, and which radiates from us as the fruit of Her presence. We know that life is most difficult when we do not feel "at home," empty within ourselves.

When we permit Sophia, the Holy Spirit, to form, renovate, decorate our "house" (our body and soul) into a home environment with Her Gifts of the Spirit, our interior and conscious self becomes peaceful and loving towards our self and everyone. We are "at home" with who we are.

That spiritual presence within us is very visible. The Shekinah of the Old Testament shines forth again as the visible manifestation of the loving presence of Sophia, the Holy Spirit. We radiate Her presence.

All the sacraments of the Church are visible manifestations of Mother Sophia's presence at that moment.

Paul told us in 2 Corinthians, 3:18, "All of us, gazing on the Lord's glory with unveiled faces, are being transformed from glory to glory into his very image by the Lord who is the Spirit." Take note that Paul said "Spirit" rather than "Jesus."

In essence, they both are One, but as persons they are distinct in their way of relating to each one within the Trinity and to all of their creation.

When we spend time in silent prayer with Sophia, the Shekinah, the Glory of the Father, we are being transformed from glory to glory in Their image and likeness by the power of Sophia. She is transforming us into Their image by love, just as a human mother does with her children in her home.

"For God, who said, "Let light shine out of darkness," has shone in our hearts, that we in turn might make known the glory of God shining on the face of Christ."

When we, men and women, live with Sophia, the Holy Spirit, it is impossible for the darkness of evil to shine through our faces. We radiate the glory of God. We radiate and share her Gifts to us. We are temples of the Sophia, Holy Spirit, where people love to come and visit. We are true Christians, Her children, filled with love.

Sophia's blessings

Our Heavenly Father, united with Sophia, created the world and all that dwells within it, including man and woman, and She, Wisdom (Sophia), danced with joy at the sight of these wonders. She blessed all of creation. She rejoiced in this holy work of the Father, her beloved spouse. There was perfect harmony in their relationship of intimate spiritual marital love.

Love of its nature needs relationships in order to grow. Love, in a sense, only exists when it is shared in some way.

Adam and Eve knew that love very well because they talked daily to God in the Garden. However, when they decided to experience separation from love they opened the door for tension and misunderstanding between them. Fear entered into their relationship. Fear vs love. John says in his epistle that where there is fear, there is no love, and where there is love, there is no fear. He called fear the true opposite of love.

There is another gift of Sophia that exists because of relationships, namely, the gift of wisdom, the ability to see how a particular item relates to everything around it. Wisdom sees how all things (seen and unseen) relate to each other. Consequently, the fruits of Wisdom are unity, life, peace, inner joy and ultimately wholeness, all of which are the work of Sophia.

Both gifts, love and wisdom, are necessary for a person's well existence as a human being. A separation or ignorance of any aspect will create fear, fear of the other, the environment in which we live and even ourselves. Both gifts are given to us at our human and spiritual birth. Wisdom is stronger in women that in men because a woman by nature is more sensitive, more sensual in her relationships with everything that exists.

A woman functions primarily in wisdom, followed by intellectual knowledge.

A man functions primarily from intellectual knowledge followed by wisdom.

When wisdom and knowledge are enfleshed with divine love that union gives us the feeling and awareness that we are "at home" with ourselves. We gladly accept who we are.

This felt wholeness is Sophia's greatest blessing for all of us. She is truly a Mother who constantly blesses with Her Love and Wisdom the Father's creation, a blessing that gives inner unity to all within. We are her children. Through this encounter with Her we are truly blessed with dignity, joy and peace. Love of its very nature brings unity, and wisdom binds it all together. These fruits of Sophia's work are always visibly.

Yes, Proverbs spoke very well of Mother Sophia's loving work among us and all the Father's creation.

In early nineteenth century a prophecy was given: "that the One who shall save us anew shall come divinely as a Woman." That Woman has to be Mother Sophia.

Come, most Holy Sophia.

Sophia's Feminine Spirituality

There are seven gifts attributed to the Holy Spirit in both the Old and New Testament: wisdom, understanding, knowledge, counsel, fortitude, piety and fear of the Lord. St. Paul attributes more, namely, healing, faith, prophecy, discernment, tongues and interpretation of tongues. All these gifts are given to us on two levels, the human and spiritual.

They do not function exactly the same in men as they do in women. They all naturally tend to relate us to God, but when the person is feminine that relationship will be expressed in a feminine way, which we have called feminine spirituality.

Feminine spirituality is more sensitive to the Divine. It is more integrated in the human life of the woman, and the fruit of this natural integration is recognized in her sensitivity towards herself, family, and the community around her. She encounters a new awareness daily as she uses her nurturing ability and her on-going life-giving gifts. Since a woman shares the same gender as Sophia, she naturally desires to relate to many things.

Woman's spirituality is tangible, enfleshed with feeling and personal connections. Some women are visionaries, probably because the female characteristics and mind of a woman are more in tune with celestial spiritual experiences of our Triune God.

Many of Mother Mary's apparitions were given to women. And many of them became well known, like, Bernadette of Lourdes, Melanie of LaSalette and Lucy of Fatima. The more a woman is united to her womanness, the more she is able to live female spirituality, which she shares with Sophia.

Wisdom in Greek is a feminine word, and without worry of error we can say that it is a natural female gift because she naturally sees and feels relationships. That's wisdom. Wisdom, as we said, is not intelligence. Wisdom sees the relationship of knowledge that is shared.

Women are also multitasking as Sophia is. (cf. Proverbs) And such an ability does not upset her ability to perform each task well.

In conclusion, Sophia is calling women to become a visible living spiritual example of Her presence within them. May all women find themselves enjoying a personal relationship with Her.

Sophia as a Mother and as a Person

All of us know "mother" from the first moment of our life. She is the first living person we experience and meet. We have no fear of mother. We learn in our early months of living that she is constantly available, and her tangible presence gives us assurance and security. Even if a mother is neither the best nor readily available, a child still desires its mother. The gift of unconditional nurturing and assistance in mothers is eternal.

However, there is the sad reality that human mothers suffer from motherhood, namely, that being mothers they are often forgotten to be a person. Many children and adults never know and experience their mother as a total person, as a woman. They only know her through her mothering.

Yes, the gift of motherhood is common to all women. It is a very special gift from which flows wonderful fruits. But, the person, as woman, who is the mother, can be missed when her feminine personhood is not tangible. If we are truly to know our mothers we must at some point in our life encounter and recognize her as a woman.

The same is true of the Holy Spirit, the third person of the Trinity. She is truly God the Mother, the one who has given life to all of the Father's creation. Yet, to keep Her locked into that precious gift of motherhood, even though it may be the most important, is to miss knowing the fuller Person, Sophia. As a Person "she delights to play with the sons of men," as she says in Proverbs. The relationship as a feminine Person is different than that as a mother.

The difference is that of love.

So, just as our relationship with our mothers must grow to also see them as a person, a woman, so also as we must grow in our relationship with Sophia, the Holy Spirit. We must come to know Her not only as Mother, the one who gives us life through the sacraments, but also as a Person, a woman, one with whom we can play and love intimately, even as a spouse. Our mothers want to be known for who they are as well as for what they do. Sophia also wants to be known for who She is as well as for what She does.

May Sophia bless us all, men and women, with the ability to see, know and honor the difference between motherhood and womanhood.

Female Spirituality

Spirituality has always existed as the work of the Holy Spirit. When the Father created with Sophia, female spirituality became evident. Sophia, the Divine Feminine, worshiped and loved the Father with all her female characteristics. She did this in perfect harmony, united to and in the Father's male characteristics. A perfect spiritual marital relationship in the Triune God. Both totally equal and yet very different in their sharing with each other.

All is done together as One, yet, in some way, the Father is the head, the leader of the Divine Family, but that does not make Him greater or more powerful than His Spouse or Son. It's the mystery of the Trinity, how Three Persons can be so intimately and perfectly One Being.

Now, we cannot forget that we are made to their image and likeness. And we express that, as men, in our masculine spirituality and, as women, in our feminine spirituality, all flowing from their image and likeness.

However, with the leaving of the Garden of Eden Adam and all men assumed the dominant role in almost all phases of human living.

He controlled the spiritual realm with his masculine spirituality by being the priest, minister, prophet and leader of all religious activities. The practice still exists today.

The woman was inferior to men in every way. A female spirituality was not spoken of, nor practiced in any open manner, and never developed into a specific rite or ritual even though it existed from the beginning.

When Jesus was presented in the temple for circumcision, it was Anna, the holy woman of the temple that recognized him as the Son of God. Even before his birth, Mary, his mother, lived in the temple and it was there that the Angel Gabriel appeared to her seeking her permission to become the mother of Jesus.

Down through the centuries, women have often grouped together to form social communities. Some groups were dedicated to minister to the community by teaching, nursing and taking care of the poor and elderly, and others, to live a quiet contemplative life dedicated to prayer and poverty. But, the spirituality that they were taught was that of the male clergy.

What is different between male and female spirituality?

Male spirituality expresses itself as linear. A man sets his sights on a goal, an objective, and he throws himself into walking that path without any deviation. He is absorbed with the need to be creative, correct and faithful to his dream that has captivated him. He will struggle and even die to maintain the course.

Female spirituality has a very different direction and objective. It is by nature cyclical. By Living a life in a cycle, they are naturally in tune with all of creation. Women are sensitive to relationships as they move through the cycle. With their sixth sense they are in tune with the orbits of heaven and earth. They are not as interested in arriving somewhere as the man is, but rather, far more interested in being present each moment to the relationship that is present as they travel the cycle.

They perceive and experience prayer, visions and relationships with God and all of creation in a sensual way. They feel the relationships of the cycle.

Female spirituality is also more directed toward the Persons of God, rather than just to God, to the persons in their human family, to themselves and the persons of the marketplace. Men go to the marketplace, for example, knowing exactly what they want. They buy it and return home. Women go to the marketplace to relate to all that is present. They may buy something, or they may not. Feeling and sensing what is present is more important in relationships.

This applies to a woman's life of prayer, which is also natural to her. As soon as she needs help, comfort and direction, she will turn to our Heavenly Father, Jesus, the Holy Spirit, the Virgin Mary (in her many titles) and/or her favorite saint and angel. She will feel assured of protection and guidance.

In other words, female spirituality not only makes one of the Persons of God visible, but also very tangible. A woman's sensual nature of feeling and experiencing makes the presence of God a living reality, one that is often experienced in celestial visions.

As we said above, many women, in order to maintain their way of living spirituality while in a masculine church, created quietly their own spirituality as they lived in religious communities.

But the vast majority of women, especially those who are married, did not have that opportunity and nothing was offered in the church community for them. The masculine church controlled how the faithful were to relate to the Triune God.

What our world needs today is the union of both spiritual paths.

Men need to acquire the wisdom of the woman's cyclical spirituality, and especially, that of Sophia, so that they will not find themselves walking over people, harming themselves or others or nature as they strive to arrive at their desired goal.

The woman, on the other hand, by acquiring some of the linear goal orientation of the men will not find themselves always going in circles that seem to lead nowhere.

We all need to experience each other's gifts for our complete development just as much as our Heavenly Father and Sophia, the Holy Spirit, need each other so profoundly in order to be One God.

May Sophia, Spirit of God and Divine Wisdom, continue to bless us with her holy insight.

Excellent Reference Books

1. <u>Sophia, Aspects of the Divine Feminine,</u> by Susanne Schaup
2. <u>The Wedding of Sophia, The Divine Feminine in Psychoidal Alchemy,</u> by Jeffrey Raff, PhD.
3. <u>Sophia, Goddess of Wisdom, Bride of God,</u> by Caitlin Matthews
4. <u>The Silent Cry, Mysticism and Resistance,</u> by Dorothee Soelle
5. <u>A Path to Divine Intimate Love,</u> by La Ermita – The Hermitage
6. <u>All Things Are United in Love,</u> by La Ermita – The Hermitage
7. <u>The Gospel of Love,</u> by La Ermita – The Hermitage
8. <u>The Odyssey of Teo,</u> by La Ermita – The Hermitage

Made in the USA
Monee, IL
06 September 2020